How to Conduct a Life in the Spirit Seminar

"A basic Presentation Guide from the Bogi Disciples of Jesus Covenant Community, Papua New Guinea"

ROMNEY CHARLES TABARA

DISCLAIMER

This publication remains the property of the St Peter the Rock sub parish, Bogi. The views and opinions expressed in this publication are entirely those of the author and are not those of the Port Moresby Archdiocese or the wider Catholic community. Neither of its members will be held liable for any loss incurred as a result of this publication. Permission will need to be obtained from the St Peter the Rock sub parish, Bogi, in order to reproduce or copy any or part of this publication.

Any queries regarding this publication can be sent to
romantabara17@gmail.com

CONTENTS

ACKNOWLEDGMENTS

The publication of this Handbook would not be possible without the assistance and support of the sub parishes in surrounding communities in Bogi, Edai, and Baruni the Erima Disciples' of Jesus Covenant Community including the local parish priest for the Hanubada Parish, Port Moresby Archdiocese, Father Justin Nenat, SVD who all participated in the Life in the Spirit seminar at the St Peter the Rock sub parish at Bogi village Lealea from 14th to 16th September 2018.

The St Peter the Rock sub-parish would also like to acknowledge the efforts of the author Mr. Romney Charles Tabara who with the assistance of all the seminar participants compiled this handbook.

FOREWORD

"This handbook is a guideline, a companion for Catholics and Non Catholics. It will help you find your way through the life in the spirit seminar and to discover all the wealth that God wants to give you. This hand book will help you to find a deeper life in God.
God speaks to us and helps us through others. If you want a new life in the spirit, you should be faithful in attending the seminar from the start to the end. God also speaks to us when we are alone, and he will do much more for us when we spend time with him during these next seven weeks and or seven days.

Prayer is simply being present with God. Our prayer can take a variety of forms. Praising and worshipping him for his own sake, thanking him for what he has done for us, asking him to do things for us or for others, listening to him to speak to us. Sometimes it is simply being quiet before him, silent in his presence.

Prayer will grow in you. At first if it is new to you, and you grow slowly. But as you come to know God more fully and experience his love, your desire to pray will increase. After you have been baptised in the spirit, you will be able to pray still more freely. God wants you to pray because he loves you and wants you to be with him. He wants to give you the gift of prayer.

The scriptures quoted in this handbook will help you to pray. They are words that God has spoken in the scriptures. He means to speak them to you now. There is one topic each day for the seven weeks and or seven days of the Seminar, and they are chosen to help you consider more deeply the material presented in the Life in the Spirit Seminar. Meditate on them each day in the time you have set aside for prayer, and the Lord will speak to you through them."
God bless,

Paul Miamel
Disciples of Jesus Covenant Community
Erima, Port Moresby
Papua New Guinea

WELCOME NOTE

"Bogi Rohodobi" the Hiri Motu word for Eagle that sits upon a tree. This majestic and noble bird much revered throughout the bible represents the characteristics of being in control, confident, dominant, assertive, cool, decisive and ambitious. A spirit we believe is alive and encapsulated in our small community of Catholic faithful.

Located in the remote Central province of Papua New Guinea along the Hiri West Highway about twenty four kilometres' outside of Port Moresby a Large Multi-National Corporation's multibillion dollar, Liquified Natural Gas Processing Plant.

The road leading to the Facility is pot hole infested and along the highway are the six main villages of Baruni, Porebada, Boera, Papa, Bogi and Lealea. Despite housing such a prominent facility, the villagers still reside in shanty houses, with no running water and pit toilets.

Here in the village of Bogi gathered under the house of local sub parish chairman are a small group of Catholic families. This is the *"St Peter the Rock sub parish"* our parish that caters to a small group of Catholic faithful in Bogi, Papa and the recently established Edai Town Housing Estate in area dominated by the Methodist or otherwise locally referred to as the United Church.

Following in the footsteps of the early apostles in the formation of the early church. Regardless, of denomination, we at Bogi seek to evangelize a message of Hope, Love, Faith and Truth to the wider community and the rest of the world through our own unique voice.

This booklet is based on our first Life in the Spirit Seminar experience which we would like to share with and bless you all.

Jacob Uda Kware
Chairman
St Peter the Rock Chapel Bogi
St Michael Parish Hanuabada
Port Moresby Archdiocese

INTRODUCTION

The Life in the Spirit Seminar is an invitation to make or renew a deeper personal commitment to Jesus Christ in openness to the Holy Spirit and its Gifts. It serves as an introduction to the power of the Holy Spirit. It provides teaching, guidance and prayer leading to a new and deeper relationship with the Lord.

The Life in the Spirit Seminar includes:
- Lively Praise and Worship
- Inspirational Speakers and Testimonies from brothers and sisters in Christ
- Discussion group sharing
- Mass
- Confession
- Prayer for release of the Holy Spirit in power
- Social Time

Whether you are Catholic, United Church, Seven Day Adventist, Baptist or any other denomination. The Lord is calling you to embrace with your heart, soul, mind and strength the teachings of the Church in the midst of this Pentecostal outpouring.

The truth we have combined with the power of the Pentecost can turn the world upside down. This movement of God is breathing renewal into the truths of the church including the following:
- Power of the Sacrament of Reconciliation

- The awesome presence of Jesus in the Eucharist
- A stirring up the Sanctifying Gifts of the Holy Spirit
- Anew depth in the use of the charismatic gift
- A renewed sense of excitement about worship and much more

The purpose of this booklet is to provide a basic guide on how to conduct a Life In the Spirit Seminar. From the 14th to 16th September 2018, we the Disciples of Jesus Covenant Community of Bogi St Peter the Rock, sub parish of the St Michael Parish, Hanuabada conducted a Life in the Spirit seminar for the first time.

It was an amazing, spirit and fun filled experience, with participants from Catholic communities in Erima, Bioto (Yule Island), Baruni, Hanuabada, and other Christian denominations one which we would like to share with you within the short pages of this book.

The aim of any "Life In the Spirit Seminar" is to renew one's experience in Holy Spirit and its Gifts. Key to this is picking a theme and related theme song for the seminar. The theme of the seminar is key to aligning all the presentations and speakers throughout the seminar. Most important of all it must be dedicated to, guided and directed by the Holy Spirit.
There are some key prerequisites before participating in this seminar, the key is preparation. Ensure you and all key speakers, participants must take part in the nine (9) novena to the Holy Spirit. This include prayer and fasting ensuring you are all fully spiritually prepared to take part in the seminar.

Adequate physical resources are essential to hosting a successful Life in the Spirit Seminar. If you are hosting a camp with several participants from afar such resources would include tents, canvas, mats, adequate camping ground, food, medicines, water supply and lighting, laptop, projector, white board, band instruments, microphones, amplifier and sound system.

TOPIC 1: GOD'S LOVE

GOAL	PRESENTATION GUIDE	DISCUSSION SESSION GUIDELINES
To attract people to the seminar, to dispose them to turn to the Lord, to begin to stir up faith in them.	**Welcome Note** **Opening Prayer** Give an overview of the presentation Personal biography a story to connect to the audience, the presenter's journey to the seminar What is God's love as defined by the scriptures, seek to identify the common themes Relate themes to ordinary and spiritual life Example of God's Love relate to the family context. **Summary and Conclusion** Scriptures to reference	*Separate into groups of five or more and have five minute discussion* *Give all members the opportunity to speak* **Points to discuss** What does God's Love mean to me? How has God demonstrated his Love in my life **Closing prayer** Nominate one member to go up and present the Group's discussion key points

GOD IS LOVE AND LOVE IS GOD

GOD'S LOVE FOUND IN
= DOING WHAT IS RIGHT/
RIGHTEOUSNESS AND TRUTH

(CREATION-GENESIS/BEGINNING) –WHEN YOU WERE BORN

(SHEPARD/EXODUS)-JOURNEY THROUGH LIFE FROM CHILDHOOD TO MANHOOD/SPIRITUAL MANHOOD

(SACRIFICE)-WHEN YOU CAME TO KNOW JESUS

(GUEST/NOW)-HE CALLS ON YOU EVERYDAY

(GUEST/NOW)-HE CALLS ON YOU EVERYDAY

(GUEST/NOW)-HE CALLS ON YOU EVERYDAY

GOD'S LOVE IS ETERNAL

TOPIC 2: SALVATION

GOAL	PRESENTATION GUIDELINE	DISCUSSION SESSION GUIDELINES
To help people see the momentousness of Christianity *To help them understand the basic Christian message (what Jesus has done and will do for them), to help them realize the need to make a serious decision.*	**Opening Prayer** Give an overview of the presentation What is Salvation as defined by the scriptures, seek to identify the common themes Nature of Sin and its Destruction The need for Salvation Examples of Salvation in Jesus Summary and Conclusion	*Separate into groups of five or more and have five minute discussion* *Give all members the opportunity to speak* **Points to discuss:** What does Salvation mean to you Have you realized the importance Salvation brings? Yes/No What should you do to be part of the Salvation of God? **Closing prayer** Nominate one member to go up and present the Group's discussion key points

SALVATION IN JESUS

The Heart, The Mind, The Soul

Are the roots of every Existing Person in the material world and in Heaven.

Where we commit our Heart & Mind determines whether our soul is worthy of Heaven or not.

Our Hearts & Minds are the place where we experience the forces of Good & Evil, Between the world of Satan & The world of Christ's Kingdom

TOPIC 3: NEW LIFE

GOAL	PRESENTATION GUIDELINE	DISCUSSION SESSION GUIDELINES
To witness to the fact that the good news is indeed good news *To let the people know that a new life is available through (a fuller) reception of the Holy Spirit, to help them to see that this new life centres in an experiential relationship with the Lord.*	Opening Prayer Give an overview of the presentation What is New Life as defined by the scriptures, seek to identify the common them Nature of Before Life and Now Life New Life in the New Testament What are the Five Holy Sacraments? Summary and Conclusion	*Separate into groups of five or more and have five minute discussion* *Give all members the opportunity to speak* **Points to discuss:** How can we get a new Life as a New Person? **Closing prayer** Nominate one member to go up and present the Group's discussion key points

WHAT IS LIFE?

Life is a Challenge	*Meet it*
Life is a Struggle	*Accept it*
Life is a Battle	*Fight it*
Life is a Problem	*Solve it*
Life is a Sorrow	*Accept it*
Life is a Burden	*Carry it*
Life is a Tragedy	*Face it*
Life is a Duty	*Perform it*
Life is a Game	*Play it*
Life is a Mystery	*Unfold it*
Life is a Song	*Sing it*
Life is a Blessing	*Take it*
Life is a Dream	*Release it*
Life is a Journey	*Complete it*
Life is a Promise	*Fill it*
Life is a Love	*Enjoy it*
Life is a Beauty	*Praise it*
Life is an Adventure	*Dare it*
Life is an Opportunity	*Avail it*

TOPIC 4: GIFTS OF THE HOLY SPIRIT AND BAPTISIM IN THE SPIRIT

GOAL	PRESENTATION GUIDELINE	DISCUSSION SESSION GUIDELINES
To help people turn away from everything that is incompatible with the Christian life and to prepare them to ask in faith for the full life of the Spirit.	**Opening Prayer** Give an overview of the presentation How do we receive God's Gifts as defined by the scriptures, seek to identify the common themes Believe, Repent and be Baptized Examples of Gifts of the Holy Spirit. Summary and Conclusion	*Separate into groups of five or more and have five minute discussion* *Give all members the opportunity to speak* **Points to discuss:** How can we obtain the gifts of the Holy Spirit? **Closing prayer** Nominate one member to go up and present the Group's discussion key points

THE 7 GIFTS OF THE HOLY SPIRIT

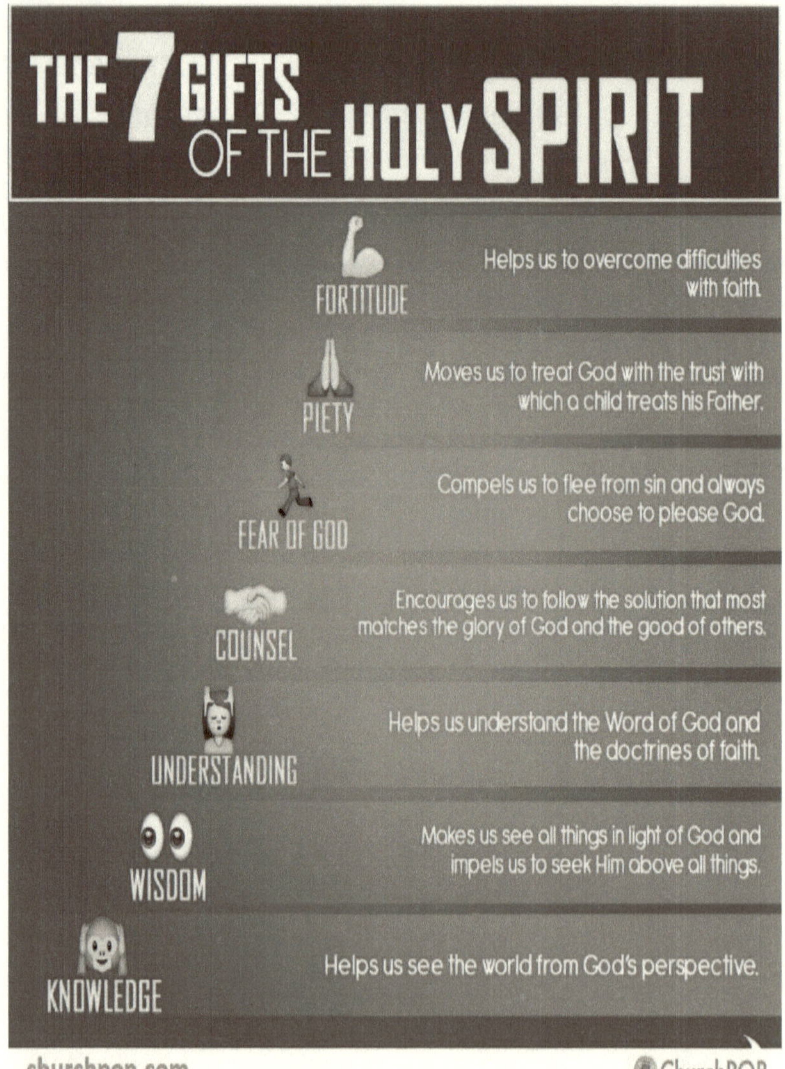

TOPIC 5: GROWTH

GOAL	PRESENTATION GUIDELINE	DISCUSSION SESSION GUIDELINES
To help them to make a commitment to take the steps they need to take to ensure they will grow in the life of the Spirit.	**Opening Prayer** Give an overview of the presentation What is Growth? as defined by the scriptures, seek to identify the common themes Physical Growth and Spiritual Growth Examples of Christian Life Wheel principle- prayer, study, service, community Summary and Conclusion	*Separate into groups of five or more and have five minute discussion* *Give all members the opportunity to speak* **Points to discuss:** How do we apply the wheel principle? **Closing prayer** Nominate one member to go up and present the Group's discussion key points

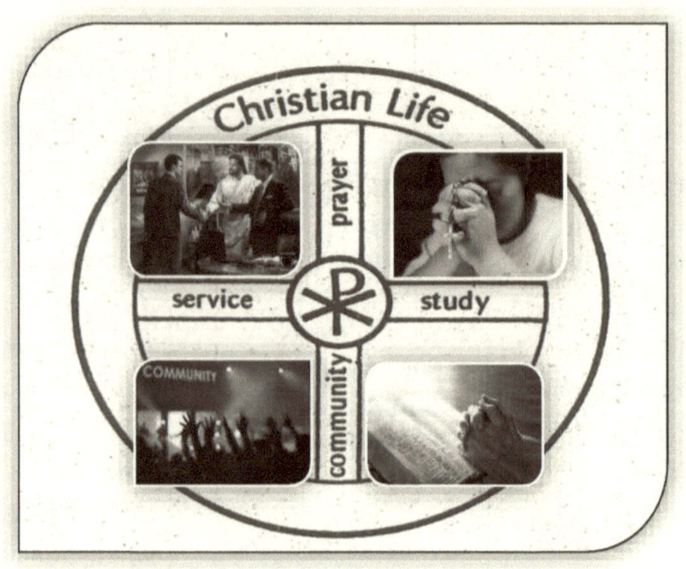

Christian Life
prayer
service
study
community
COMMUNITY

TOPIC 6: CONFESSION AND RECONCILIATION

GOAL	PRESENTATION GUIDELINE	DISCUSSION SESSION GUIDELINES
To help them come back to God all whom have been strayed by sin.	**Opening Prayer** Priest to give an overview of the presentation Different names of sacrament-conversion, penance, confession, forgiveness and reconciliation Examples of different degrees of sin-mortal sin, venial sin, social sin Summary and Conclusion	*Separate into groups of five or more and have five minute discussion* *Give all members the opportunity to speak* **Points to discuss:** How do we apply penance in Christian life? **Closing prayer** Nominate one member to go up and present the Group's discussion key points

THE 7 HOLY SACRAMENTS OF THE CATHOLIC CHURCH

THE SEVEN SACRAMENTS

My name is ________________________________

BAPTISM

Baptism takes away original sin, all personal sins and removes any punishment due to sin. It gives our souls the new life of grace and makes us children of God.

Color the Baptismal Font and write the name of the church and the date of your Baptism:

____

____

CONFIRMATION

In Confirmation the Holy Spirit gives us His gifts and power to help us grow to be strong Christians. The Bishop anoints us with "chrism" oil to serve God and others. Write the names of the gifts of the Holy Spirit in the flames above.

HOLY EUCHARIST

The Holy Eucharist is the Body and Blood of Jesus. When we receive Holy Communion we are united more closely to Jesus and we grow in love for God and others.

CONFESSION

In Confession we confess, or tell, our sins to a priest. God forgives our sins through the priest and fills us with grace and joy to help us obey Him and do what is right.

Draw yourself going to Confession and write down something for which you are truly sorry.

____

MATRIMONY

The sacrament of Matrimony unites a man and a woman together as husband and wife. It gives them a special grace to live for Jesus and to fulfill the duties and dignity of marriage.

HOLY ORDERS

In Holy Orders, bishops ordain men to become bishops, priests, or deacons. God gives these men special graces and power to serve Him and others.

Write the name of your parish priest and pray one Hail Mary for him every day.

____

ANOINTING OF THE SICK

In the Anointing of the Sick, the priest anoints the sick person with blessed oil and lays his hands on them for healing, strength, peace, and courage. This Sacrament also forgives sins if the person is not able to go to Confession.

TOPIC 7: TRANSFORMATION IN CHRIST

GOAL	PRESENTATION GUIDELINE	DISCUSSION SESSION GUIDELINES
To help people avoid discouragement over problems they experience, and to help them become part of a charismatic community or prayer group.	Opening Prayer Give an overview of the presentation Summary of all previous topics discussed What is Transformation-how to grow in Christian Life; and how to make the connection necessary in order to keep growing in the Spirit; Example of the journey of the patriarchs 40 years and 40 days preparation principle Summary and Conclusion	*Separate into groups of five or more and have five minute discussion* *Give all members the opportunity to speak* **Points to discuss:** Difficulties and trials experienced in Transformation **Closing prayer** Nominate one member to go up and present the Group's discussion key points

PRINCIPLE OF 40 DAYS OF TRANSFORMATION

WHAT IS THE SIGNIFICANCE OF **FORTY** DAYS?

Archdiocese of Toronto

www.archtoronto.org
archtoronto

Source: *The Lent, Triduum and Easter Book* by Paul Niemann

SUMMARY, REFECTIONS AND CONCLUSION

The Life in the Spirit seminar run at the St Peter the Rock parish was a spectacular three day event filled with love, fun, joy and entertainment.

Once all the sessions have been completed the Priest is to conduct a final mass to conclude the seminar and bring everything into perspective, Participants in this particular seminar included groups from Legion of Mary; Erima, Roku, Baruni, Edai Town, Bogi and Hanubada and other Four Square Gospel Church, United Church and the Salvation Army Church.

Some of the Key Remarks made by some of participants included:

Topic 1: "God's love must be present in the family, you need not look elsewhere" Romney Tabara, Edai Town.

Topic 2: *We must experience Salvation in Jesus through heart, mind, and the soul* Tasi Uda, Bogi

Topic 3: *New Life is a journey, enjoy it in Christ* Jacob Uda, Bogi

Topic 4: "Gods gifts must be shared according to God's timing", Celestine Aumpoa, Erima.

Topic 5: *"The wheel must always be spinning it needs a driver to constantly turn it,"* *Aida Tabara, Edai Town.*

Topic 6: "Penance are key to your walk and growth in the Christian faith, specifically the cycle of sin, confession, and reconciliation." Fr Justin Nenat SVD

Topic 7: *"Transformation-it's a mindset-think, walk, talk and believe," Thomas Base, Edai Town.*

REFERENCES

ChurchPOP Editor (2018), *The 7 Gifts of the Holy Spirit*, www.churchpop.com

Niemann, P. (1998) *The Lent, Triduum and Easter answer Book*, San Jose, California: Resource Publications

Uknown Author, (2018) *The Life in the Sprit Seminars Team Manual,* Disciples of Jesus Covenant Community, Erima Parish, Port Moresby

www.autom.com

PHOTO GALLERY
LIFE IN THE SPIRIT SEMINAR
BOGI

AUTHOR NOTE

The Author of this book, Romney Charles Tabara is a Catholic convert and a Senior Human Resource Management and Training Development Professional having served extensively in Government and the Public Service. This short but simple presentation is based on a first time 'Life in the Spirit Seminar' that was conducted in Bogi, in the remote Central Province of Papua New Guinea in 2018.

We thank you for reading this book which has been quite a struggle to publish due to a lack of proper publishing, editing and author support facilities in Papua New Guinea, including high internet costs and low connectivity issues.

I even had to go to the extent of opening a virtual foreign currency account because unfortunately Papua New Guinean bank accounts are not recognized on Amazon. A very challenging journey even for producing self-published book.

This is my first attempt at writing a book, with others in various genres soon to follow. As part of my service to the Church and putting the Good Lord first in all things we do. We present this book for you readers to give you small glance into bringing the Gospel into this isolated part of the world.

Funds raised from the sale of this book will go towards constructing our chapel here at Bogi. We thank you for reading this book and pray that it does enrich your life.

Please do provide a review and may the Lord bless you in the name of the Father, Son and the Spirit.

Amen.

www.ingramcontent.com/pod-product-compliance
Lightning Source LLC
Chambersburg PA
CBHW051336160726
47995CB00004B/1108